The Complete

of

CATHERINE Parr

The Learned Queen's Journey Through Faith and Power

Inkline publishing

Inkline Publishing

All rights reserved. No part of this work may be reproduced, distributed or transmitted in any form or by any means, including photocopying, recording, or other electronic or mechanical methods, without the prior written permission of the copyright owner.

Copyright ©Inkline Publishing, 2024.

Inkline Publishing

Table of Contents

Introduction 4
A Daughter of the Gentry 8
   Family Origins and Early Years 8
   Social Status and Upbringing 11
A Woman of Learning 14
   Education and Intellectual Pursuits 14
   Religious Beliefs and Personal Convictions 16
Early Marriage and Court Life 18
   Marriages to Edward Burgh and John Neville 18
   Experiences in the Tudor Court 20
Henry's Last Wife 22
   Marriage to King Henry VIII 22
   Navigating the Role of Queen Consort 24
A Queen of Letters and Faith 28
   Catherine Parr's Literary Works 28
   Influence on the Protestant Reformation 30

Copyrighted Material.

- A Queen in Widowhood 34
  - Life After Henry VIII's Death 34
  - Role in the Regency for Edward VI 36
- The Admiral's Wife 40
  - Marriage to Thomas Seymour 40
  - Challenges and Controversies 41
- The Last Days of Catherine Parr 44
  - Final Years and Passing 44
  - Legacy and Historical Impact 45
- Beyond the Crown 48
  - Catherine Parr's Enduring Influence 48
  - Cultural and Historical Reflections 50
- Conclusion 54
  - Summarizing Catherine Parr's Legacy 54
- Biography 58
  - Sources and Further Reading 58

INTRODUCTION

"I am but a weak and sinful woman, yet, I have been blessed with the strength to stand in the light of truth."

Imagine a woman in a world where her voice was expected to be silent, where her ambitions were meant to be contained. Think of this woman defying these expectations, seeking knowledge and finding expression when women were largely silent.

That woman was Catherine Parr, the last queen of Henry VIII.

Her story is one of courage and quiet strength. She was not merely queen; she wasn't just an ordinary wife. She was a knowledgeable person, someone who loved books and truth. She wanted more than the luxury of life that comes with royalty such as silk garments and expensive jewelry; she desired to explore ideas, theology, and write at length.

Through her journey towards power she came close to Henry himself. And even in that turmoil marriage, she held onto herself believing in what she thought was right for her own sake. She could risk being a Protestant in a kingdom struggling with religious change. She dared for learning institutions for all denied persons thereby opening the door for education.

But destiny is a hand of cruelty. Her husband's death left her without a mooring, in a time when women were expected to just kind of fade away. Not Catherine. She became powerful herself, emerged as an advocate for Protestantism, and protected her stepson the young king.

And then love happened. She loved someone who was like her, someone who pushed her boundaries and filled her days with desire.

But they were short-lived happinesses. Tragedy again came knocking and Catherine had to endure yet another heartbreaking experience.

It is not just about the queen I'm talking about here. It is more than that; it is also a story of a woman who dared to dream or a woman who refused to let others define them. It is also the story of an intellectual, mother, wife, and only women who found power within themselves against all odds.

I want you to come with me now on this journey down history's path. Let us embark on this voyage into Catherine Parr's life: where she succeeded and failed; what made her happy and what scared her most? Above all things we must seek out this woman whose life was so extraordinary it continues to inspire us today even as we live our own lives.

Inkline Publishing

Inkline Publishing

A DAUGHTER OF THE GENTRY

"The grace of God is the fountain of all goodness, and from whence proceedeth all virtue."

....Catherine Parr

Family Origins and Early Years

What if the worth of a woman was gauged by her capability to find a man to marry, bear children for and take care of the household? That's the world that Catherine Parr was born into. A world she would later defy but first she had to learn its rules.

She was born into an average family, the daughter of a gentlewoman. Even though her parents were not rich, they loved education. Those were moments in life that one never forgets; imagine how precious it must have been when Catherine as a young girl, together with her siblings were literate when they read books about history or learnt religion difficulties through those quiet times. She grew up to be a woman who yearned for information and also refused to allow herself to be limited as was typical of women during her time.

Her early life was full of laughter and anecdote, yet there were also strains in the family as they sought to survive during a crackdown on heresy promoted by Henry VIII. The world was ever changing, religion a fluid thing and yet their own home had no escape from the unknown.

On the other hand, Catherine Parr had always been a child who found strength in books, one who sought solace in knowledge. This little girl grew up around people who loved education or her family encouraged curiosity.

The beginnings of her life may have been curtailed by the limitations of her age but they laid the foundation for a lady who would eventually defy those constraints; far above any expectations that could be placed upon her being a woman.

Moreover, we will now consider these critical years as we go forward with this story. The importance of learning has played out since she was young which became manifest through her strong character nurture throughout her entire life and accomplishments. It shows how families can influence lives forever and those early years remain significant as magical moments when girls are allowed to be curious about anything while finding comfort through books.

Social Status and Upbringing

Catherine Parr as a young girl grew up in a world where a woman's worth was measured by her family's standing and her ability to secure a good marriage. She was a gentlewoman's daughter, not a noblewoman, so her life was filled with the quiet comfort of a modest estate, but also the awareness of social limitations.

It's easy to visualize those early years, filled with the gentle rhythm of family life, but also with the ever-present whispers of societal expectations. She saw the world for what it was, a world where women like her were expected to be seen and not heard. But she also sensed the possibility of something more, a world beyond the confines of her social status.

Catherine Parr's upbringing may have been defined by those limitations, but it also nurtured a quiet determination within her. She saw the power of education, the strength that came from knowledge. And, as we explore her story, we'll witness how those early experiences fueled her desire to break free from the mold, to forge a path of her own, a path that led her from a gentlewoman's daughter to a woman who defied the expectations of her time.

Inkline Publishing

A WOMAN OF LEARNING

"The knowledge of God hath showed me the way of truth, and brought me out of darkness and error."

.... Catherine Parr

Education and Intellectual Pursuits

Catherine Parr distinguished herself as an exceptional woman of learning during a time when formal education for women was not commonly emphasized. Born into a noble family, she had access to a robust education that included classical studies, languages, and the arts. Catherine was proficient in Latin, French, and Italian, languages that were essential for engaging with the rich literary and philosophical works of the Renaissance. Her education was not merely for display; she was a serious scholar who enjoyed deep intellectual engagement.

Her intellectual curiosity extended beyond languages. Catherine was an avid reader, particularly interested in theology, history, and classical literature. Her personal library contained numerous books, reflecting her wide-ranging interests. This breadth of knowledge allowed her to engage in the vibrant intellectual debates of her time, making her a respected figure among scholars and theologians. As queen, Catherine fostered an environment of learning at court, encouraging the study of humanist ideals and supporting the work of contemporary writers and thinkers.

Religious Beliefs and Personal Convictions

Catherine's intellectual pursuits were closely intertwined with her religious beliefs. She was a committed Protestant and a fervent advocate for the English Reformation. Her religious convictions were shaped by her belief in the accessibility of Scripture to the common people, a principle that led her to support the translation of the Bible into English. This belief was a bold stance during a period of significant religious tension and persecution.

Catherine's devotion to her faith was not just theoretical but practical. She authored several religious texts, including "Prayers or Meditations" and "The Lamentation of a Sinner." These works provided spiritual guidance and reflected her deep theological understanding. Catherine's writings emphasized personal piety and the importance of a direct, unmediated relationship with God, bypassing the traditional ecclesiastical hierarchy.

Her influence extended beyond her personal writings. Catherine played a significant role in the religious education of Henry VIII's children, particularly Elizabeth and Edward, who would later ascend to the throne. Her efforts ensured that the future monarchs were well-versed in Protestant doctrine, significantly shaping the religious landscape of England.

Catherine Parr's commitment to learning and her unwavering religious convictions marked her as a pioneering figure of her time. She navigated the complexities of the Tudor court with grace and intelligence, leaving a lasting impact on the cultural and religious fabric of England. Through her intellectual pursuits and deep faith, she demonstrated that women could be both scholars and spiritual leaders, setting a powerful example for future generations.

EARLY MARRIAGE AND COURT LIFE

"The life of man is short, and subject to many miseries, troubles, and adversities."

.... Catherine Parr

Marriages to Edward Burgh and John Neville

Catherine Parr's early marriages played a significant role in shaping her experiences and preparing her for her future role in the Tudor court. Her first marriage, to Edward Burgh, was arranged when she was still a young woman. Edward was a member of a prominent northern family, and the union was a typical example of the strategic alliances made among the nobility during that era. Unfortunately, Edward's health was poor, and their marriage was short-lived; he passed away in 1533, leaving Catherine a widow at a young age.

Following Edward Burgh's death, Catherine married John Neville, 3rd Baron Latimer, in 1534. This marriage elevated her social status and provided her with a more prominent position within the noble hierarchy. Baron Latimer was significantly older than Catherine and had two children from a previous marriage, whom she helped to raise. This role offered her valuable experience in managing a household and navigating the responsibilities of stepmotherhood.

Catherine's marriage to Latimer brought her closer to the center of Tudor politics. Latimer was implicated in the Pilgrimage of Grace, a significant uprising against Henry VIII's religious policies. Although Latimer himself was not a leader of the rebellion, he was coerced into participating, which placed the family under considerable scrutiny. Catherine demonstrated resilience and diplomacy during this period, helping to protect her husband's interests and maintain their family's safety. This experience gave her a firsthand understanding of the volatile nature of Tudor politics and the precariousness of noble life.

Experiences in the Tudor Court

Catherine Parr's entry into the Tudor court came with her marriage to John Neville, who was a nobleman with connections to the royal family. Her position provided her with a unique perspective on the political and social dynamics of the time. While she was not yet in the inner circle of the court, she observed the complexities of court life and the shifting allegiances that characterized the reign of Henry VIII.

During her time at court, Catherine honed her skills in diplomacy and discretion, qualities that would prove invaluable later in her life. She witnessed the intrigues and power struggles that defined the Tudor court, as well as the harsh consequences faced by those who fell out of favor. These experiences likely shaped her cautious approach to court politics and her understanding of the importance of aligning with the king's interests.

Catherine's marriages to Edward Burgh and John Neville were formative in her development as a figure of influence. They provided her with crucial insights into the workings of the nobility and the court, laying the groundwork for her eventual role as queen consort. Her ability to navigate the challenges of her early marriages and her experiences in the Tudor court demonstrated her resilience and intelligence, qualities that would come to define her legacy.

HENRY'S LAST WIFE

"God hath called me of his great mercy to be a defender of his truth."

.... Catherine Parr

Marriage to King Henry VIII

Catherine Parr's marriage to King Henry VIII on July 12, 1543, marked a significant chapter in her life, placing her at the center of Tudor England's complex and often dangerous political landscape. As Henry's sixth and final wife, Catherine entered a marriage that was less about passion and more about mutual respect and companionship. By this time, Henry was aging and suffering from a variety of health issues, making him a challenging spouse. Despite the risks associated with marrying a king notorious for his turbulent marital history, Catherine accepted the role with grace and a sense of duty.

Catherine's experience and maturity set her apart from Henry's previous wives. Having already been twice widowed, she understood the intricacies of noble life and the weight of responsibility that came with it. Her marriage to Henry wasn't about producing an heir, as Henry's children from previous marriages were already grown. Instead, Catherine provided Henry with comfort and care, becoming a steady presence during the final years of his reign. Her deep commitment to Protestantism also aligned with Henry's religious reforms, solidifying her position at court.

Navigating the Role of Queen Consort

As queen consort, Catherine Parr had to navigate the complexities of court life, balancing the demands of her role with the expectations of a volatile king. She quickly proved herself to be a capable and intelligent queen, engaging in theological debates and participating in the governance of the kingdom. Catherine's intellect and education were assets, allowing her to contribute meaningfully to the discussions and decisions of the time. When Henry went to France for military campaigns, he appointed Catherine as regent, demonstrating his trust in her abilities.

Catherine's influence extended beyond politics. She played a crucial role in the lives of Henry's children—Mary, Elizabeth, and Edward—by fostering a nurturing environment and advocating for their education. Her efforts to reconcile Henry with Mary, who had been estranged due to the fallout from Henry's previous marriages, showcased her diplomatic skills. She also left a lasting impression on Elizabeth, who would later become one of England's greatest monarchs. Catherine's emphasis on education and her Protestant faith significantly shaped Elizabeth's views and policies.

However, Catherine's time as queen was not without challenges. Her outspoken support for Protestantism nearly led to her downfall when conservative factions at court sought to undermine her. In a dramatic episode, she narrowly escaped arrest by skillfully convincing Henry of her loyalty and devotion, thereby securing her position. This incident highlighted Catherine's quick thinking and political acumen, traits that were essential for survival in the treacherous world of Tudor politics.

Catherine Parr's role as Henry's last wife and queen consort was marked by her intelligence, compassion, and ability to navigate a complex and often dangerous court. She left an indelible mark on history, not only as a caretaker and partner to Henry but also as a reformer and advocate for education and religious reform. Catherine's legacy endures as a testament to her strength and resilience in a time of great uncertainty and change.

Inkline Publishing

A QUEEN OF LETTERS AND FAITH

"The light of the gospel bringeth more light, and discovereth the secret workings of Satan."

.... Catherine Parr

Catherine Parr's Literary Works

Catherine Parr distinguished herself not only as a queen but also as a woman of letters, contributing significantly to English literature and religious thought. As a prolific writer, she was the first English queen to publish works under her own name, a remarkable achievement in a time when women's voices were often marginalized. Her literary output reflects her deep intellectual engagement and theological insight, addressing both spiritual and moral concerns.

Catherine's most notable works include "Prayers or Meditations" (1545) and "The Lamentation of a Sinner" (1547). "Prayers or Meditations" is a collection of devotional texts designed to guide readers in their personal spiritual practices. It emphasizes the importance of prayer and reflection, offering a structured approach to daily devotions. The work was widely read and appreciated, reflecting Catherine's ability to articulate complex religious ideas in an accessible manner.

"The Lamentation of a Sinner," published posthumously, is an autobiographical confession of faith. In this work, Catherine reflects on her own spiritual journey, expressing profound remorse for her sins and a deep commitment to Protestant ideals. The text is a powerful testament to her personal piety and theological understanding, providing a unique glimpse into her inner life. It also underscores her belief in the doctrine of justification by faith alone, a cornerstone of Protestant theology.

Influence on the Protestant Reformation

Catherine Parr played a pivotal role in advancing the Protestant Reformation in England. Her writings and actions reflected a deep commitment to the principles of reform, particularly the accessibility of religious texts and the importance of personal faith. Catherine was an ardent supporter of translating the Bible into English, making it accessible to the common people. This effort was aligned with the broader Reformation movement's goal of democratizing religious knowledge, allowing individuals to engage directly with the Scriptures.

Her influence extended beyond her writings. As queen, Catherine was a patron of reformist scholars and theologians, providing them with protection and support. She fostered a court environment that encouraged religious debate and the dissemination of Protestant ideas. Catherine's patronage helped to spread reformist thought, positioning her as a key figure in the religious transformation of England. Her support of Protestantism also had a significant impact on the royal family. Catherine played a crucial role in the religious education of Henry VIII's children, particularly Edward VI and Elizabeth I, both of whom would become prominent Protestant rulers. Her efforts ensured that Protestant teachings were imparted to the future monarchs, shaping their religious policies and the course of English history.

Catherine Parr's legacy as a queen of letters and faith is marked by her intellectual contributions and unwavering commitment to the Protestant cause. Her writings provided spiritual guidance and theological insight, while her actions at court helped to advance the Reformation. Catherine's influence on the religious landscape of

England was profound, making her a significant figure in the history of the English Reformation.

Inkline Publishing

A QUEEN IN WIDOWHOOD

"God is the protector and defender of the widows, and will not leave them comfortless."

....Catherine Parr

Life After Henry VIII's Death

The death of Henry VIII on January 28, 1547, marked the end of Catherine Parr's turbulent tenure as queen consort, but it was far from the end of her story. As a widow, Catherine faced a new set of challenges and opportunities, navigating her life with grace and resilience. Her mourning for Henry was both a personal and political necessity, yet it was not long before she began to shape her own destiny, free from the constraints of an often-dangerous marriage.

Catherine's transition to widowhood was accompanied by a profound sense of relief and renewed purpose. Freed from the intense scrutiny and demands of being Henry's wife, she turned her attention to her personal interests and relationships. One of the most significant aspects of her post-royal life was her relationship with Thomas Seymour, brother of Jane Seymour and uncle to the young King Edward VI. Catherine and Thomas had known each other for some time, and their mutual affection led to a swift and somewhat controversial marriage, conducted in secret just a few months after Henry's death.

While her marriage to Seymour brought personal happiness, it also introduced new complications. Seymour was ambitious and somewhat reckless, and his actions often placed Catherine in difficult positions. Despite these challenges, Catherine remained steadfast in her duties and responsibilities. She continued to care for her stepchildren, particularly Elizabeth, who lived with her and Seymour for a time. Catherine's influence on Elizabeth during this period was profound, as she provided the young princess with a nurturing environment and access to an excellent education. Catherine's own experiences and intellectual pursuits served as an inspiration to Elizabeth, who would later ascend to the throne as one of England's greatest monarchs.

Role in the Regency for Edward VI

Catherine's role in the regency government for Edward VI was both unofficial and yet significant. While she did not hold a formal position in the regency council, her influence was felt in various ways. As the widow of Henry VIII and stepmother to the young king, Catherine possessed a unique combination of personal authority and political insight. Her experience as queen consort had equipped her with a deep understanding of the complexities of court politics and the delicate balance of power required to govern effectively.

Catherine's influence was particularly evident in the realm of religious policy. As a committed Protestant, she supported the continued advancement of the Reformation under Edward VI's rule. She remained a patron of reformist scholars and continued to write and publish works that advocated for Protestant theology. Catherine's presence in the young king's life provided a stabilizing influence, helping to guide him through the early years of his reign.

Tragically, Catherine's life was cut short not long after she gave birth to her only child, a daughter named Mary, in August 1548. She died on September 5, 1548, likely from complications related to childbirth. Her death was a significant loss, not only to her family but also to the broader political and religious landscape of England. Catherine Parr's legacy, however, endures. Her contributions to the English Reformation, her literary achievements, and her role in nurturing the future Elizabeth I are lasting testaments to her intelligence, compassion, and resilience.

In widowhood, Catherine Parr demonstrated that she was more than just a queen consort; she was a woman of substance and strength, whose impact extended far beyond her marriage to Henry VIII. Her life after his death reflects a journey of personal growth and a continued commitment to the ideals she held dear. Catherine's story is one of perseverance and courage, a testament to the enduring power of faith and intellect in the face of life's challenges.

Inkline Publishing

Inkline Publishing

THE ADMIRAL'S WIFE

"A new chapter in life is not without its trials, but it is also filled with opportunities for growth and discovery."

Marriage to Thomas Seymour

After the death of Henry VIII, Catherine Parr found love again with Thomas Seymour, the dashing and ambitious younger brother of Jane Seymour, Henry's third wife. They had known each other for some time, and it was rumored they had feelings for each other even before Catherine married Henry. Just a few months after Henry's passing, Catherine and Thomas secretly wed, much to the surprise and gossip of the court.

Their marriage was a fresh start for Catherine. She had spent much of her life navigating the complexities of royal marriages, and with Thomas, she seemed to find a sense of personal happiness. They moved to Sudeley Castle, where Catherine continued her role as a caregiver and mentor, particularly to Elizabeth, who was in her early teens and lived with them for a while. Catherine's influence on Elizabeth was significant, as she provided a loving and intellectually stimulating environment for the future queen.

Challenges and Controversies

However, Catherine's marriage to Thomas was far from smooth sailing. Thomas was known for his ambitious and often reckless nature. He had big dreams of gaining power and influence, but his methods were questionable. One of the biggest controversies came when Thomas began to flirt with young Elizabeth, leading to rumors and suspicions about his intentions. This situation put Catherine in a difficult position, as she had to manage the delicate balance between her husband and her beloved stepdaughter.

Thomas's actions didn't stop there. He continued to pursue power, even attempting to get closer to the young King Edward VI. His behavior eventually led to his arrest for treason in 1549. During this tumultuous time, Catherine was pregnant with their first child. She gave birth to a daughter, Mary, in August 1548, but tragically, Catherine died shortly after, likely from childbirth complications.

Catherine's marriage to Thomas Seymour was a whirlwind of emotions and events. While it brought her personal happiness, it also exposed her to new challenges and controversies. Thomas's ambitions ultimately led to his downfall, but Catherine's legacy as a loving and intelligent woman who cared deeply for her family remained intact. Despite the drama and difficulties, she left a lasting impression on those around her, including the future Queen Elizabeth I.

THE LAST DAYS OF CATHERINE PARR

"O Lord, let my soul rejoice in Thee, and rejoice in Thy mercy."

Final Years and Passing

The final days of Catherine Parr's life were bittersweet. After her marriage to Thomas Seymour, she hoped for a new beginning, away from the shadows of Henry VIII's court. At Sudeley Castle, she embraced the chance to live a quieter life, focusing on her new family and the joy of expecting her first child. The anticipation of welcoming a daughter was a bright spot in her life, and on August 30, 1548, Catherine gave birth to a beautiful baby girl, whom she named Mary.

But the joy of motherhood was fleeting. Just days after giving birth, Catherine fell seriously ill with what is now believed to be puerperal fever, a common and dangerous infection for women after childbirth. Despite the best care available, Catherine's condition worsened rapidly. The vibrant woman who had been a pillar of strength and wisdom at court found herself slipping away. On September 5, 1548, Catherine Parr passed away, leaving behind a grieving husband and a newborn daughter who would never know her mother's loving touch. She was just 36 years old, and her death was a heartbreaking end to a life full of promise and perseverance.

Legacy and Historical Impact

Catherine Parr's legacy is deeply moving and inspiring. As the last wife of Henry VIII, she was more than just a consort; she was a woman of profound intellect and faith. Catherine was a pioneer in many ways, becoming the first English queen to publish works under her own name. Her writings, particularly "The Lamentation of a Sinner," revealed her deep personal faith and her journey towards spiritual enlightenment. Through her words, Catherine opened her heart to the world, sharing her struggles and beliefs, and leaving behind a powerful testimony of her convictions.

Her influence extended beyond her literary contributions. Catherine was a loving stepmother to Henry's children, especially young Elizabeth. She provided a nurturing and intellectually stimulating environment, guiding Elizabeth and helping shape her into the formidable queen she would become. Catherine's impact on Elizabeth's education and faith was profound, instilling in her a love for learning and a commitment to Protestantism. This influence undoubtedly played a role in Elizabeth's future policies and the stability she brought to the kingdom during her reign.

Catherine's dedication to the Protestant cause was another significant aspect of her legacy. She was a passionate advocate for the

Reformation, using her position to promote the translation of the Bible into English and to support Protestant scholars. Her efforts helped to spread Protestant teachings and solidify the religious transformation in England, making her an important figure in the country's spiritual history.

In the end, Catherine Parr's life was a testament to resilience and grace. She faced immense challenges, from navigating the dangerous politics of the Tudor court to enduring the personal losses of her many marriages. Yet, she remained steadfast in her beliefs and compassionate in her actions. Catherine's legacy is one of a remarkable woman who left an indelible mark on history, not only as a queen but as a mother, a writer, and a woman of faith. Her story continues to resonate, reminding us of the strength and courage it takes to remain true to oneself in the face of adversity.

Inkline Publishing

BEYOND THE CROWN
"All things here are but temporal, and soon shall have an end."

Catherine Parr's Enduring Influence

Catherine Parr's legacy extends far beyond her role as the sixth and final wife of Henry VIII. Her enduring influence is felt not only in the realm of politics and religion but also in the broader cultural and intellectual landscape of England. Catherine was a woman ahead of her time, whose intellect, compassion, and unwavering commitment to her beliefs have left an indelible mark on history.

As a writer, Catherine Parr broke barriers, becoming the first English queen to publish works under her own name. Her writings, such as "Prayers or Meditations" and "The Lamentation of a Sinner," were not just personal reflections but also significant contributions to the religious discourse of the era. These works offered spiritual guidance and expressed her Protestant faith, at a time when the English Reformation was still evolving. Catherine's theological insights and her ability to communicate complex religious ideas in an accessible manner made her an influential figure in the Protestant movement. Her writings provided a framework for personal devotion and introspection, which resonated with many during a period of profound religious upheaval.

Beyond her literary achievements, Catherine played a crucial role in shaping the future of the Tudor dynasty. Her influence on the young Elizabeth I was particularly significant. As Elizabeth's stepmother, Catherine provided a nurturing and intellectually stimulating environment that helped shape Elizabeth's character and beliefs. Catherine's emphasis on education and her commitment to Protestantism left a lasting impression on Elizabeth, who would go on to become one of England's most iconic and successful monarchs. Catherine's guidance during Elizabeth's formative years was instrumental in preparing her for the challenges she would face as queen.

Cultural and Historical Reflections

Catherine Parr's life and legacy offer rich material for cultural and historical reflection. She lived during a pivotal moment in English history, a time when the country was grappling with religious change, political intrigue, and social transformation. Catherine's story provides valuable insights into the complexities of life at the Tudor court and the challenges faced by women in positions of power.

Culturally, Catherine Parr represents a bridge between the medieval and early modern periods. Her advocacy for the education of women and her own scholarly pursuits were progressive for her time, laying the groundwork for the gradual expansion of opportunities for women in intellectual and public life. Catherine's legacy as a learned and articulate woman challenges the often limited and stereotypical portrayals of women in history, highlighting the diverse roles women have played in shaping society.

Historically, Catherine's contributions to the English Reformation and her role in the consolidation of Protestantism in England cannot be overstated. She was a key figure in promoting the translation of religious texts into English and making them accessible to the broader public. Her support of reformist scholars and theologians helped to advance the Protestant cause and secure its place in the English religious landscape. Catherine's efforts in this regard were not only a reflection of her personal beliefs but also a significant factor in the broader movement towards religious reform in England.

In conclusion, Catherine Parr's life and legacy go beyond her status as a queen consort. She was a woman of profound intellect, courage, and faith, who navigated the complexities of her time with grace and determination. Her enduring influence is evident in the realms of religion, education, and cultural history. Catherine Parr's story is a testament to the power of intellect and conviction, and her contributions continue to be a source of inspiration and reflection for those interested in the rich tapestry of England's past.

Inkline Publishing

CONCLUSION

"Let us be remembered not for the grandeur of our titles, but for the strength of our character and the depth of our convictions."

Summarizing Catherine Parr's Legacy

Catherine Parr's legacy is one of remarkable resilience, intellect, and grace. As the last wife of Henry VIII, she played a pivotal role in the tumultuous final years of his reign, navigating the complexities of court life with wisdom and tact. Yet, Catherine's influence extended far beyond her role as queen consort. She was a pioneering author, a devout Protestant, and a compassionate stepmother to Henry's children, particularly

Elizabeth, who would carry forward many of Catherine's teachings and values.

Catherine's literary contributions, including "Prayers or Meditations" and "The Lamentation of a Sinner," were groundbreaking, making her the first English queen to publish under her own name. These works were not only expressions of her deep faith but also important contributions to the religious discourse of her time. Her commitment to Protestantism and the education of women were progressive stances that helped shape the religious and intellectual landscape of England.

Culturally, Catherine's life serves as a bridge between the medieval and early modern periods, challenging contemporary norms and expanding the roles available to women in intellectual and public spheres. Her support for the English Reformation and her role in the education of the future Elizabeth I were significant factors in the development of England's Protestant identity.

In summary, Catherine Parr was a woman of exceptional character and influence. Her legacy is a rich tapestry woven from her contributions to literature, religion, and education. She stands out as a figure of strength and conviction, whose impact resonated far beyond her lifetime. Catherine Parr's story is a testament to the enduring power of intellect, compassion, and faith in shaping the course of history.

Inkline Publishing

Inkline Publishing

BIOGRAPHY

Sources and Further Reading

To gain a comprehensive understanding of Catherine Parr's life and impact, a variety of sources and scholarly works offer valuable insights. Here are some key resources for further reading:

1. **"Catherine Parr: Henry VIII's Last Love" by Linda Porter**
   This biography provides an in-depth look at Catherine Parr's life, exploring her roles as queen consort, widow, and reformer. Linda Porter delves into Catherine's personal and political struggles, offering a detailed portrait of her character and achievements.

2. **"The Wives of Henry VIII" by Antonia Fraser**
   Antonia Fraser's book includes a detailed examination of Catherine Parr among Henry VIII's other wives. Fraser's work

provides context on Catherine's marriage to Henry and her influence within the Tudor court.

3. **"Catherine Parr: The Sixth Wife of Henry VIII" by Michael Jones**
Michael Jones offers a focused exploration of Catherine Parr's life, particularly her marriage to Henry VIII. The book sheds light on her experiences and the political landscape of the time.

4. **"The Life and Times of Catherine Parr" by David Loades**
David Loades provides a thorough account of Catherine Parr's life, including her contributions to literature and religion. This book is a valuable resource for understanding her broader impact on English history.

5. **"The Reformation of the Church of England" by Geoffrey Elton**
For a broader understanding of the religious context in which Catherine Parr

operated, Geoffrey Elton's work provides insights into the English Reformation and its key figures, including Catherine.

6. **Primary Sources**
Catherine Parr's own writings, such as "Prayers or Meditations" and "The Lamentation of a Sinner," are essential for understanding her personal beliefs and theological perspectives. These texts provide direct insight into her intellectual and spiritual life.

These resources collectively offer a rich tapestry of information about Catherine Parr, her life, and her lasting influence on English history. Whether you are interested in her personal journey, her role in the Reformation, or her literary contributions, these works provide a comprehensive view of one of history's remarkable women.

Inkline Publishing

Printed in Great Britain
by Amazon